Heaven's Playground

Story by Theodora Higgenbotham

Illustrations by Tianna J.Palmer

ISBN-13: 978-0692089910

Note:

Scriptures used from Psalms: Poetry on Fire
(The Passion Translation - Psalms 104)

How to Use This Book

Heaven's Playground is a storybook and an interactive activity book. On selective pages are black and white line drawings. If you choose to, you are to color the images using crayons or colored pencils. On the final page, there is a black and white border to color, and to place a photo of your loved one.

Dedicated to the memory of our dearly beloved, who are in Heaven.

You are sitting and thinking about loved ones who are now in heaven and imagine how heaven would look. Immediately, you hear a soft whisper, say, "Come along and see."

You are teleported onto a fluffy white cloud that resembles your favorite toy.

Bouncing on the
wings of the wind,
you sweep through
the air, being lifted
higher and higher
into the bluest sky.

Looking down, you see fruit bearing trees, a happy man wearing a crown of gold who joyously leaps mid-air. Around Him are children sparkling like stars, singing, and dancing.

"Guardian Angel," you ask, "Is that Heaven's King playing with the shining boys and girls?"

"Yes. He is our Majestic King. He plays with His children in heaven's glowing light."

On wings of the wind, your cloud
swoops you, higher, higher.

You see giggling children riding on
their colorful fluffy toy shaped clouds,
zig - zagging, whooshing - whizzing
through heaven's bluest skies.

They see you and beckon, "Come!"
You follow, listening to their happy
songs of praise to Heaven's King.

The wind blows gently, carrying the melody of another alluring song. Your new friends and you swoop down and hover above the shimmering ground. "Look," Angel's friend calls and points and shouts, "The King sings."

Horses, lions, tigers, monkeys, camels, elephants and many land creatures come to listen to the King's song and eat from the King's soft hands.

Bounding above the clear waters, you see
sharks, seals, dolphins, and whales riding
the waves, coming to hear the King's song.

"Guardian angel," you ask, "In heaven do
all creatures sing?"

"Yes," your Guardian Angel answers, "All creatures great and small, sing praises to our Heavenly King."

You see bright, colorful birds' wings flap to the rhythm of the King's song as they fly around fragrant flowering fruit trees.

You see the King, and He sees you. He waves, smiles, and calls you by name. With glee-filled-laughter, the King shouts, "Enjoy your visit on Heaven's Playground."

His enormous feet stand on two ruby red majestic mountains. Beneath Him flows sparkling, clear water.

He scoops the cold, fresh water into His loving hands as creatures great and small come to drink.

Your cloud gently glides through the air and then settles down on the greenest grass.

Bright and colorful crystal-like butterflies' flutters, in perfect formation. Bumble bee's flit from flower to flower, humming their songs of praise to the King.

The vibrant and colourful flowers, sing in unison, growing and shining, moving to heaven's endless rhythmic melodies. You think, "Everything in heaven lives and sings!"

You hear, "*Come and play.*"

You turn to see happy angels spiraling down cascading rainbow waterfalls. Soaring, ascending, descending, effortlessly in and out of sprouting floating fountains.

You see angel nannies with children, dancing, rising above the blue, green grass, nestled inside sparkling, swirling crescent-moons.

You see nannies sitting on twirling gemstone benches. Shimmering star children swing on exquisitely decorated swings floating in the spacious skies.

You see sparkling children dance to the sounds of uplifting beats, pulsating out of the gold covered moving grounds.

The trumpet's sound blasts in the sky. The King of Heaven appears wearing a decorative purple robe, riding on a stately white horse draped with sparkling diamonds.

"Let us go," whispers your guardian angel.
"Where to?" you ask.
She responds, "To the King's banquet."

Your guardian angel opens heaven's pearly doors. There, standing, in front of His fiery gemstone rainbow throne, now dressed in a flowing, exquisite, gold, and purple robe, cheerfully welcoming everyone is the King of Heaven.

The King's laughter releases His Spirit's wind. You hear many languages and somehow you understand every word.

All the guests sit with the King at an enormous bejeweled banquet table laden with scrumptious delicacies. We eat until filled. Then, the King sings, and we dance inside heaven's radiant paradise.

Dancing, spinning, like a Merry-go-round. You stop. You see family members and friends who have left you on earth, but now dwell in heaven with the King.

They, too, see you, then wave, and smile. Quickly, you turn towards your loved ones. Your guardian angel takes hold of your hand and says, "It is time."

"Time?" you repeat.
"Yes, it's time for you to return home."
You do not want to go. You want to stay with your family and friends and play forever on heaven's playground.

The King of Heaven hears your cry and sees your tears. He takes your hands, and says, "I understand you wanting to stay but your time will come. It will not be today.

"You have many more remaining years on earth; some days will be happy; some days will be sad. Some choices you make will be good, and some bad.

"Throughout your years, months, weeks, and days, up until the very end, stay connected to Me and love Me with all your heart.

"**A**nd when your day comes to see heaven again, I will be waiting and watching from the skies' lofty portal to hear your sound of praise.

"**I** will not be able to hold my joy. I will come swiftly, whirling, around and around, swirling on an arched rainbow, to fly with you into the bluest skies, and together we will travel through worlds without end on Heaven's Playground."

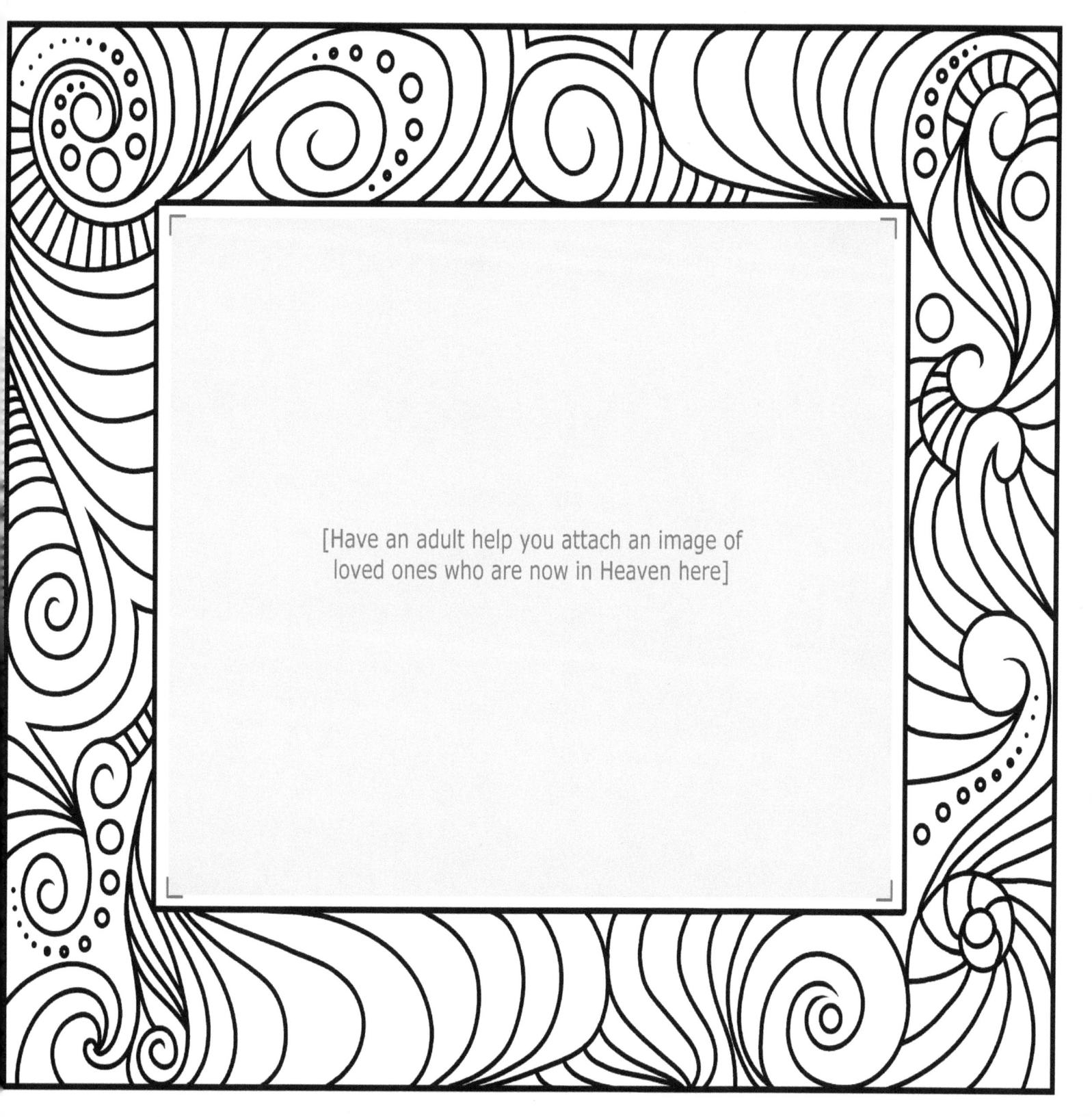

[Have an adult help you attach an image of loved ones who are now in Heaven here]

ABOUT THE AUTHOR

Theodora Higgenbotham is a retired public-school teacher and an active minister on the Healing and Prophetic team in her church. She attended Aenon Bible College and a graduate of Columbus School of Supernatural Ministry (CSSM). In addition, she holds a B.A. in Education from Ohio Wesleyan University, a M. Ed in Curriculum Design and is a past recipient of The Ashland Oil Outstanding Teacher Award and a Martha Holden Jennings Foundation recipient.

Theodora has published three other books: This Little Pin Dot, and a planned trilogy with two parts already published: *Part 1: Lies, Secrecy, and Deceptions* & *Part 2: Lies, Secrecy, and Deceptions Divulged.* Part 3 is planned for a 2019 release.

In her spare time, she contributes to her blogs:

Theodora's Inspirational Thoughts and *Living Insight on the Word of God.* Theodora's favorite scripture is Psalms 37: 4-5.KJV

She has been married for 37 years and has two children.

ABOUT THE ILLUSTRATOR

Tianna J. Palmer is a self-taught artist and life-long Christian. Though she began with traditional art, particularly pencil and paper, she now mostly draws digital art through an electronic art tablet straight onto her computer. Born in Ohio on October 15th, 1995, having no professional art training, Tianna instead learned on her own and by spending time with artistic family members and friends. Her youth was filled with sketching horses, other animals, and nature. Family travels and fun brightened her childhood with adventure and learning about God kindled her spirituality. Over the years her friendship with Him only grew deeper.

God leads Tianna with a brightly colored palette and spiritual marvel through her work and life. He's been the inspiring voice in many of her unpublished novels and novelettes over the years, of which much of her art nowadays depicts scenes and characters from. An adventurous spirit, Tianna aspires to travel the world and explore the Earth's cultures while spreading God's love and truth. Through her works, travels, and relationship with God she wants to not just talk about his glory but show it. She's a chaser of modern miracles and a seeker of inspiring the hearts of people. She desires to continue growing spiritually, toning her art skills, learning more of who God is, and spreading his beauty and identity to the world through her art, stories, and wherever she may walk.

www.ingramcontent.com/pod-product-compliance
Lightning Source LLC
Chambersburg PA
CBHW042118040426
42449CB00002B/93